My Good Friend

by Nina Valenti
Illustrated by Don Dyen

PEARSON
Scott Foresman

Editorial Offices: Glenview, Illinois • Parsippany, New Jersey • New York, New York
Sales Offices: Needham, Massachusetts • Duluth, Georgia • Glenview, Illinois
Coppell, Texas • Sacramento, California • Mesa, Arizona

Hi! My name is Sasha, and I have a story to tell. One Friday morning in September, our teacher, Mrs. Ferrara, told us that a new student was joining the class.

"Her name is Luz," said Mrs. Ferrara. "She is transferring from the Lakeland School. She is interested in math and music. You might notice that Luz doesn't see in the same way most people do."

Luz walked into our classroom Monday morning. She was using a folding cane. I think she used it to make sure her feet would not bump into things. Ms. Ferrara gave her a seat in front of the room. Her desk was far from the window. Maybe the glaring light near the window bothered her.

---

folding cane: special cane, or walking stick, that folds and becomes smaller

Mr. Timms came in with a small computer that had a special light. He put it on Luz's desk. I found out later that the type on the screen looked large. Then he brought in a piece of equipment that Luz used to make the type in a book look big.

Some of the children wanted to help Luz get in line for lunch. She refused quietly, “Thanks, but I don’t need help.”

José tried to help her walk downstairs to lunch, but again she answered, “Thank you, I don’t need help.”

I introduced myself at lunch. “Hi, Luz, I am Sasha, and I came from Russia last year.” She responded softly, “Hi, Sasha. I was born in California, but my parents are from Mexico.”

Luz seemed to be avoiding us. I thought she looked a little sad.

One day, I dared to ask. "Why are you sad, Luz?"

She looked at me and didn't say anything for a moment. Then she said, "I miss my friends from my old school. They knew me already. They knew what I could do. They knew when I needed help and when I didn't."

avoiding: staying away from

dared: had the courage

In October, things began to get better. It was time for chorus to begin practicing. Luz and I both joined. Luz had a great voice!

When clubs were announced, Luz selected Math Club. She was a math whiz! Soon Luz was helping other kids in the class who struggled with math. Luz looked happier now. She talked more.

chorus: a group of people who sing songs together

Luz became very special to me. We talked and shared our secrets during recess. We visited after school. Sometimes on weekends, our families went out together. We became best friends. I could tell Luz anything. She could keep secrets. She sure was a good friend!

Extend Language **Verb Endings: *-ed, -ing***

*help**ed*** and *help**ing*** are forms of *help*

*miss**ed*** and *miss**ing*** are forms of *miss*

Can you make new words by adding *-ed* and *-ing* to the following verbs? Use a sheet of paper.

Verb	*-ed* form	*-ing* form
look		
talk		
avoid		